LIGHT AND SHADOW

DOODLE AND PECK PUBLISHING
YUKON, OKLAHOMA

ISBN# 978-0-9966205-7-4 (hard cover)
ISBN# 978-1-7323637-6-2 (soft cover)

©2016 Howard F. Stein

All rights reserved. No part of this book may be reproduced in any form or by any electronic or mechanical means including information storage and retrieval systems without permission in writing from the publisher, except by a reviewer, who may quote brief passages in review.

Publisher:
Doodle and Peck Publishing
P.O. Box 852105
Yukon, OK 73085
www.doodleandpeck.com

Library of Congress Control Number: 2016939548

Manufactured in the United States of America

Dedicated to my Friday Afternoon Writers' Group—
Jeannie Hagy, Sandi Lawson, Marla Jones, Susan Meyers, Una Belle Townsend,
David Barrow, and Dorothy Shaw

TABLE OF CONTENTS

Foreword

Introduction

Poems

~In Nature's Realm~
Geology Lesson
Cerro Pedernal
Urgency
The Stream
Preparation
Awaiting the Next Season on the Prairie
Cottonwood Ode
The Return
Spring Procession
Early Dog Days
Awaiting Sundown on the Prairie
Among the Leaves
Autumn Polyphony
Cathedrals
Cornflower Blue
Winter Arrives
The Duality of a Tree

TABLE OF CONTENTS, continued

~Our Handiwork~
Watch the Winter Wheat
David Levine's Prairie Farm Photographs
Prairie Panorama, Photo by David Levine
The Ballad of the Chainsaw
Transformational Leadership
Invisible
Who We Are
At the Airport Gate
Hello! Hello!
Is There an Earth?
Evolution

~Life, Love, and Loss~
Ingrid's Pantry
Sly Hope
Waiting
Nine Lights
Sky High – Winter, 2013
Useless Keys
Disappointment
Extinguished
Odds
Turning
Body Hunger
Cliché
Convoluted
After You Died
Life Is Not a Straight Line

Other Books of Poetry by Howard F. Stein

Prairie Voices
Evocations
Learning Pieces
Sketches on the Prairie
Theme and Variations
From My Life
Seeing Rightly with the Heart
In the Shadow of Asclepius: Poems from American Medicine
Raisins and Almonds

LIGHT AND SHADOW

BY HOWARD F. STEIN

Foreword

Howard Stein offers the reader an opportunity to intimately experience nature, life, and the workplace. We all share in common events that evoke deep feelings, some not fully understood or appreciated, and some forgotten to time, but still very present. These experiences may be filled at times with pleasure and joy, and at other times more darkly with pain and suffering, that are often put away in our minds, but always there. Howard's poetry encourages reflection and a deeper sense of knowing.

Stein's poems are evocative, informative, and most importantly allow us to understand that we are not alone in this experience, as if to say, "I know that," and, "I lived through that." These poems are a metaphoric window into self-insight, empathy for others, connection with the majesty of nature and the universe, and perhaps in some small measure an opportunity to work through the experience of our lives. They are to be experienced, enjoyed, embraced, and perhaps, most of all, felt.

Seth Allcorn

Introduction

In this life, whenever light encounters an object there results a shadow. Life is an eternal dance between light and shadow. Sometimes one seems to prevail over the other. But light and shadow are inseparable. They are the warp and weft of a lifetime's fabric. This book of poetry offers portraits of both from many vantage points. No one poem has the final word. The final word is the eternal dance of light and shadow.

Howard F. Stein
26 February 2016
Oklahoma City, Oklahoma

Geology Lesson
for Ed Knop

Plateau,
mesa,
butte,
pinnacle,
chimney rock,
cap rock –
surfaces of the past,*

sedimentary layers
iced with hard lava,
eons that give
a new slant to our ambition.
Here time stands still
not even a second.
Water, ice, and wind
have work to do,
proclaiming their sovereignty
over geology's fleeting majesty.

Still, I marvel,
knowing full well
that erosion is just
another word for time.

*phrase from Alyssa Tomalino, 7/11/15, e-mail, used with permission

Cerro Pedernal

A mountain
nested in a bed of cottonwood,
a perfect partial frame,
happenstance of perspective
across an alfalfa field.
Stubby, flat-topped volcano,
prized by Georgia O'Keefe,
once hers, now mine.
She painted; I write.
This, an inexhaustible mountain,
never twice the same.
I never know when
the Pedernal will surprise me again,
a welcome ambush,
always there to greet me
upon my eager return.

Urgency
Ghost Ranch, New Mexico

I study the mesa's face —
its blinding afternoon brilliance;
its ever-changing,
ever-vanishing colors
in evening;
the lone juniper lodged
in a fortuitous crevice.
My thirsty eyes drink in
what will soon
vanish into memory
and dissolve into night.

The Stream

Neither particle nor wave,
a stream is pure time,
has no desire but to flow.

It carries dirt;
it cures driftwood;
it cuts through rock.

A stream bows
only to gravity,
taking with it
where it has been
to where it is going,
and picks up more
along the way.

A stream says
where it is going –
it never asks.

"If a stream winds through all this…
it will not
Say where it has been."
John Ashbery. A Wave. New York: Viking Press, 1985. P. 31.

Preparation

Everything is preparation,
each moment, seeds
of the next, tiny acorns
on oak branches in mid-spring,
two seasons from fruition.

Pastel green in early spring
unfolds and darkens into
hearty summer foliage.
Autumn's bright reds and golds
utter protest against
barren branches and winter's rest –
prologue to sun's awakening rays
and soon to be broad oak leaves
sheltering mature acorns,
harbinger of fall's biting chill.

Each season gives way
to its successor –
a curving line that
eventually meets itself.
Each end a beginning.
Each beginning an end.

Awaiting the Next Season on the Prairie

It is always like this —
in the oppressive heat of summer,
rain so intermittent
so as to bring to mind drought,
we long for the cool days of fall,
bright yellow leaves on cottonwood,
soft sweater and cozy wood fire —

but forget
cascading autumn rains,
flooded pastures and streets,
tractors stuck in mud,
killing frost on lovingly tended
roses and marigolds —

heedless, too, as the sun sets,
of children's summer play,
gleefully splashing in backyard hose-fountains,
evening cookouts, lazy lounging
on the front porch, with sweet tea
and conversation.

Next season will be better,
will redeem us from the woes
of this one, a nostalgia
for the future that never comes.
It is always like this.

Cottonwood Ode
for Ed Knop

Along a streambed,
cottonwood roots claw deep
in search of water,
for when the stream cracks dry.
Their trunks' tough bark,
a mail of armor, fends off
wind and rain, snow and ice,
and unforgiving summer sun.

Leaves shimmer brilliant yellow
against the autumn prairie sky.
Majestic cottonwood –
a silent tale of survival and victory,
written in wood and leaf,
in a land that makes no promises.

The Return

Like a magnificent
spray of fireworks,
my roses returned
after a six-month absence.
I could not tell
whether the bare stalks
signaled death or dormancy.
Nor could I account
for so abundant
a regeneration.
Was it the plant food,
the rain, the pruning?
The wishful anticipation?
I have always had
a scientific turn of mind,
but I am not
beyond bafflement
and simple gratitude
when what
might be readily explained,
appears with so large
a tincture of surprise.

Spring Procession

As predictable as sunrise,
as regular as the tides,
in an ancient cadence
jonquils and daffodils
poke their heads through
the last winter snow;
a riot of trees dressed in white;
forsythia bursting in yellow;
redbud brilliant in lavender and red;
azaleas just in time for Easter.
Finally, enter the laggards of spring —
scrub oak, post oak,
hickory, and cottonwood,
the last to venture out.
Soon, in procession towards summer,
everything turns green,
all nature in its time.
Season upon season,
year upon year,
the cycle repeats.

I begin with expectation,
but end with astonishment.

Early Dog Days

July rather than August—
cloying air and oppressive sun;
sweat beads and runs in rivulets
over exposed skin,
then drips to the ground.
A hot southwest wind
thrusts hot dust
into nose and mouth.
Movement becomes languid, effortful.
Will everything melt
and flow like Dali's watches?
Summer's dog days
arrived early this year.

Awaiting Sundown on the Prairie

Supple leaves shrivel
and crispen in the heat.
Broiling, baking—
in the sky-oven
no cloud to hide under
for man, woman, or cow.

The sun-flame
broils grass,
broils land,
broils skin.

A fierce southwest wind
drives dust into the eyes,
makes grit in the mouth.

Sundown cannot come
soon enough.

We call the hour evening,
but the sun still
has two hours left in the sky
before earth's rotation
gives us reprieve
until morning and more sun.

Among the Leaves
for Phil Floyd

Gusts of cool wind
push in from the north,
pull brown and yellow leaves
off their branches,
sending them down
in a soft, diagonal rain.

I sit on my small porch,
coffee mug in hand;
leaves swirl all around me;
they transfix my gaze.
I dwell amid the post oak
and blackjack, inside
this ancient dance.

I do not observe –
I participate –
wrapped in a comforter of leaves.

Autumn Polyphony

A brisk north wind shakes
yellowed scrub oak leaves,
translucent in late day sun.
Those freed from their branches,
dart about and dive in brisk breeze.
Boughs weave up and down
like the rhythm of an old wooden metronome.
On the ground, squirrels scout acorns,
chittering and chasing each other into trees –

all this, a kind of polyphony,
many voices singing their lines
simultaneously on nature's tall staves.
My eyes see autumn.
My ears hear Bach.
Even at this late hour,
there is music to savor.

Cathedrals

Leaves on arching branches
of scrub oak
glow translucent gold
toward sunset in mid-autumn.
For a moment, the gleaming
vault seems to hover.

Had I not leaned backwards
as far as I could
and looked straight up,
I could have missed
this miracle
of transience and light.

Cornflower Blue

Between sunset and dusk,
an autumn prairie sky
settles into a hush
of cornflower blue.
It lingers as I walk alone
on an old dirt road,
wraps itself around me
as a faint chill alights
onto the land below.

Vast beyond measure,
this hue
appears in the sky
one season a year,
is good to look forward to,
is good to remember,
is good to envelop myself in —
this cornflower blue
time of year.

Winter Arrives

Winter declared itself today
with rude finality.
Relentless cold rain and wind
tore the last reluctant leaves
from scrawny scrub oak.
Bare branches cut spectral figures
against the gray, bone-chilling afternoon.

Heedless of any calendar,
winter stole the stage.
"I arrive when I please,"
winter decreed to its shivering audience,
who put on their heavy coats
and left the theater
for biting wind, howling trees,
and a perilous trip home.

It was a simple matter
of who was sovereign
and who was subject.

The Duality of a Tree

I sit on my porch, smoke my pipe,
not enough of a breeze
to put out a match.
My trees comfort me,
silent companions
this quiet late fall day.

I'd rather not think how
two weeks ago an ice storm
strangled even the largest limbs
till they snapped and crashed,
smashed roofs and struck the ground.
Those friendly trees
quickly turned on me,
menaced my home,
and ripped all wire connections
with the outside world,
as I waited for the next branch to pop
in the black of night –

not so easy to reconcile
trees who can be
reassuring presence one minute
and dreadful peril the next –
how to transmute this duality
of friend and foe into
the thought of a single tree?

Watch the Winter Wheat

Watch the winter wheat grow,
seed in furrowed dirt;
the faintest hint of green
in perfectly parallel rows;
a lawn of deep green;
for a time, pasture
for hungry cows in winter,
if snow is not too deep;
rising in spring dark green
until heads form,
and grass turns to grain;
broad, golden waves in the wind,
as perfect as the narrow rows last fall;
then watch, wait, hope, and pray
the wheat will not be
beaten to death by hail,
drowned and rotted by too much rain,
starved to death by too little;
then, having cheated death
by grace or luck,
wheat is ready for cutting.

I could spend a lifetime
watching winter wheat grow.

David Levine's Prairie Farm Photographs

Photographs of farms,
taken from a great distance,
are all of a piece.
They tell the same story
over and again
so that it might sink in.

The farms – houses, barns,
silos, sheds, implements,
horses, cattle –
crowd the bottom of the picture,
miniatures in the face of the sky
who rules from above.

Long-approaching storms,
tornadoes, deluges and droughts,
snow and ice, wind that is almost a person,
and the blessed, accursed sun –
farm and farmer give homage
to their dominion.

Prairie sky puts human striving
at the bottom of its great canvas.
Farmers never cease to turn
their gaze upon the endless
and endlessly changing sky.
For them, the sky is never empty.

Successful harvest
is more luck than plan.
Farming is a gamble –
and the sky always wins.

Prairie Panorama, Photo by David Levine

A scene from the High Plains —
it is easy to get lost in this picture.
From where the photographer stands,
the distant farm is a miniature.

Two small houses, three squat silos,
and a blurry outline of a few trees
stand alone against the far horizon.
Washed-out brown straw fields
and a narrow road
separate photographer from farm.

The rest is sky, a vast gray-blue
with few thin filaments of white clouds.
There is comfort in remoteness,
where deep sky and uninterrupted land
are the only neighbors. Here isolation
is solace, not empty desolation,
and any intrusion can be seen
long before it arrives.

These farming folk are not lost in space —
they know exactly where they are.
They belong.

The Ballad of the Chainsaw

Chainsaws buzz, sing, shriek
throughout the neighborhood,
throughout the day, long into evening –
following two days of freezing rain
that wrapped itself around
branches huge and small;
then sounds of crack, pop,
crash, limbs onto roofs or
on the frozen ground.
Trees split like celery stalks,
the region resembles
a tornado's wild swath,
but here half a state wide.
Little here to call beauty
on sun-blinding glassy branches
that sagged, drooped,
and snapped with a gun's report.

Newscasters speak of resilience—
we sing the ballad of the chainsaw,
one limb at a time,
only slowly reclaiming our wounded world,
unable to rid ourselves
of the surreal amputation
we witnessed for two relentless days.
We relive it in our minds—and saw on.

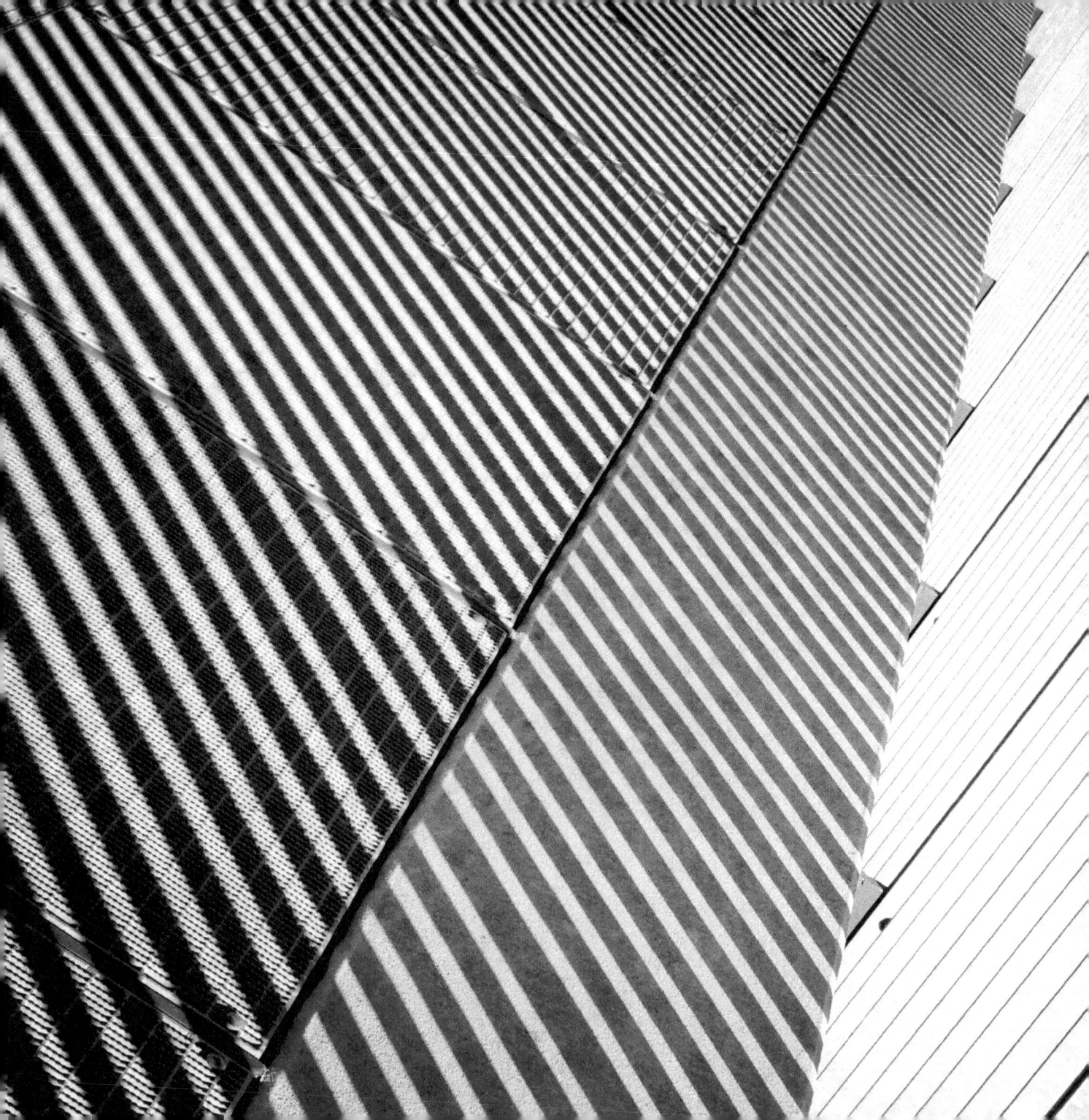

Transformational Leadership

The new CEO
arrived with a flair,
like a god on a chariot,
this shaman of change.
He followed Nietzsche's dictum,
that "great creators must
be great destroyers,"
Shiva in the flesh.
He drilled down his will
into the soul of the organization,
replacing their thought
with his thought,
until only his thought remained:
one corporation,
one mind,
one will,
lockstep awe,
the culture a cult,
a divine kingship.
His power glittered as the gold
of productivity,
of profit,
of perfection,
a well-oiled machine
submitting to only one machinist.
Besides him
there is
no corporation.
There is only "I."

Invisible

Leaden words
wooden words
magical words
recited like an incantation

    downsize
    rightsize
    RIF
    redundant
    restructure
    reengineer
    outsource
    offshore
    deskill

words for the pain
unacknowledged by those
who inflict it
and by those lucky enough
to have survived
until the next wave

                                                                                      people disposed of
like trash for profit
not folks but figures
lives ground into dust
hopes and dreams
livelihoods and worlds

turned out into the street
forgotten (Did they ever work here?),
sacrificed on the altar
of the Sacred Shrine
of the Bottom Line.

Who We Are

A matrix of sacred clichés
proclaims to the world,
"This is the way
we do things around here –
don't mess with it."
We don't dream of
thinking outside the box.
We are the box.

At the Airport Gate

Airport terminal, Gate B 13,
I sit alone amid the din.
Passengers wait and talk
into their cell phones,
stare spellbound at computer screens,
scroll feverishly on their smart phones,
eat and drink their purchases
from fast food stalls between gates,
glance quickly
at whoever is around –
no eye contact allowed.
Travelers walk the halls – some run –
to and from airplanes.
Airport nomads in queues seek assurance
that they're at the right gate.

This place could be an Edward Hopper painting,
except here, everyone eventually moves,
some slowly, some frenzied,
all wayfarers passing through.

I sit and daydream, close my eyes,
breathe slowly and deeply.
I disappear into my sanctuary
and stake my claim
on solitude before I fly.

Hello! Hello!

Voice to voice, so good
after all these months
of you in the form
of electrons on a screen,
representations of you
as strings of words
that can vanish from
the mere pressing
of Delete or Back Space.
For that matter, I could
select your entire e-mail
and make you disappear.

We don't even call
our conversation
a letter any more –
those old fashioned
hand-written pieces of paper,
enclosed in an envelope
arriving in our mail box,
brought by a mail man.
At least I could touch the paper.

But on the telephone,
it is so good to hear
your voice –
almost three-dimensional,
with pitch and tone,
volume and musicality,
breath and sigh.

Voice to voice is so good –
almost like being with you.

Is There an Earth?

So many ways to say
who I am: my religion,
my nation, my state, my city,
my town, my neighborhood,
my farm, my party, my company –
unlike those who live
across the railroad tracks
across the highway,
across the sea,
or across the city
in another glass tower.
We're the only real human beings,

My world is *the world*,
the only one that exists for me,
the only one I can imagine.
There is no earth –
only what is mine and ours.

Who thinks of the earth?
After all our hate,
our smoke,
our beslimed waters,
will there be an earth left?
Who speaks for the earth,
pearl of the seas,
giver of life?

Will there be an earth left,
or is it already
an afterthought?
Has the clock
already struck midnight?

Evolution

Who speaks for the earth,
that ocean blue speck
in the spiral arm
of an unremarkable galaxy?

Why are we so eager
to find life elsewhere
that we squander the gift
we have here been given?
Will any other planet
offer us sanctuary?
Would we spoil it, too?

With what gratitude
do we spew our contempt
for earth's frailty
into the air and into the seas?
What hatred have we for our nest,
as we anxiously prize
over all else
the next quarterly report?

What animal have we become
who makes this blessed home
our accursed tomb?

Ingrid's Pantry

In two weeks the German bakery closes.

You would never know
from the giant glass window strip mall front
the cavernous Old World likeness inside.
Framed prints and posters of Germany,
France, and Italy adorn simple yellow
plaster walls.

Glass-enclosed refrigerated
cabinets display pastry, cakes, and pies.
The sweet scent is the Jewish bakery
of my long-ago childhood half a continent away.
The staff welcome me as if I belong.
The place is vast, the pastry divine,
unlike anything supermarket bakeries make.
Despite the shop's size, I feel cozy here.
I bring my writing, have a sandwich
and strudel or chocolate pie, then set to work.

Two weeks from now the search
for a new home begins —
today, I'll have another piece
of pie.

I mourn the loss of this place,
for to be a Jew at home is no small thing.

Sly Hope

Sly hope,
furtive hope.

Just when I
gave you up for dead,
you return
like Til Eulenspiegel*
to haunt me,
badger me,
remind me
that what I thought
I longed to be rid of
I fervently wish to keep.

Sly hope,
furtive hope.

I grieved what
seemed to be
lost forever,
only to find
it has again
taken up residence
and refuses to leave.

Hope, you are a Trickster
toying with my heart.

*Til Eulenspiegel is a picaresque character from medieval German folklore, who played pranks, was full of mischief, exposed wrong-doings, and was utterly predictable.

Waiting

the letter that does not arrive
the phone that does not ring
the e-mail that is not received
the door that no one knocks at

spring without blossom
leaf without flower
wish without fruition
time without fulfillment

waiting without end
longing without rest

Nine Lights

Across the way, my neighbor's lights
sparkle in the ice and snow,
pierce the terrible spring storm,
appear when chilling night first falls,
relieve the desolation of summer heat.
I look out my window;
my neighbor's lights
comfort me.
Each night, I peer through my venetian blinds
and count the nine lights that stand sentinel
before my neighbor's house.
I tell myself I am safe;
I can lower my guard;
I can let myself sleep.
I have told my neighbor
I feel protected by his lights;
I thank him for his gift.
One last time, before I get in bed,
I check that my nine lights are still there –
my lighthouse on the coast of despair,
whose sea pounds the shore
with relentless waves of fear.
But sometimes, even nine lights
are not enough to stem the tide.

Sky High – Winter, 2013

Three months of pneumonia,
aggravated asthma,
gasping for my next breath;
inhaling miracle mist from a nebulizer,
to open lungs
and calm the fear of suffocation.
But what price relief?
I soar sky high for at least an hour –
fueled by medicine,
I could fly to the moon.
Restless, agitated, can't sit still,
can't lie down, can't concentrate.
I am a wild animal.
Never having tried mind-altering substances,
I imagine this is what it would be like.
After days of frenzied distraction,
for the frantic hour after each treatment,
I fancy putting this madness to use:
do the laundry, iron clothes, wash the dishes,
vacuum the house, correct student papers,
pay monthly bills, keep busy, busy, busy –
until at last, the side effect
wears off; and, exhausted,
I finally breathe freely and sleep,
dreaming now of winter delights.

Useless Keys

Useless keys
conjure time,
open doors
to places long gone.

Useless keys
fit nowhere now,
but once took me
somewhere I knew.
What does it matter that
the connection is lost?
The keys —
they are the treasure
that stores time for me.

Useless keys —
are they?

Disappointment

Did you give me hope,
or did I simply hope too much?
Was impossible ever possible?
Did I just dream too much?
Finding and being found
are such a happenstance thing,
it's a wonder lovers ever meet.

Extinguished

Fire has long departed
from this old hearth.
No phoenix will rise
from these cold ashes.
Skeletal remains
of burned-out wood
lie lifeless in the bed
of crumbled coals.
Nothing left to do
but shovel the pit clean
and gather fresh wood.

Odds

Statistics are against it.
Probability says to give up.
Reality counsels me
to forget the whole idea.
Still, I dream
that you might appear
and I be restored to life –
against all odds.

Turning

Many women
turn my head.
But you're the one
who turns my heart.

Body Hunger

the yearning
to be touched
by hands that mean it
by hands that want to touch

the longing for hands
to release the skin
from solitary confinement
and a sentence of death

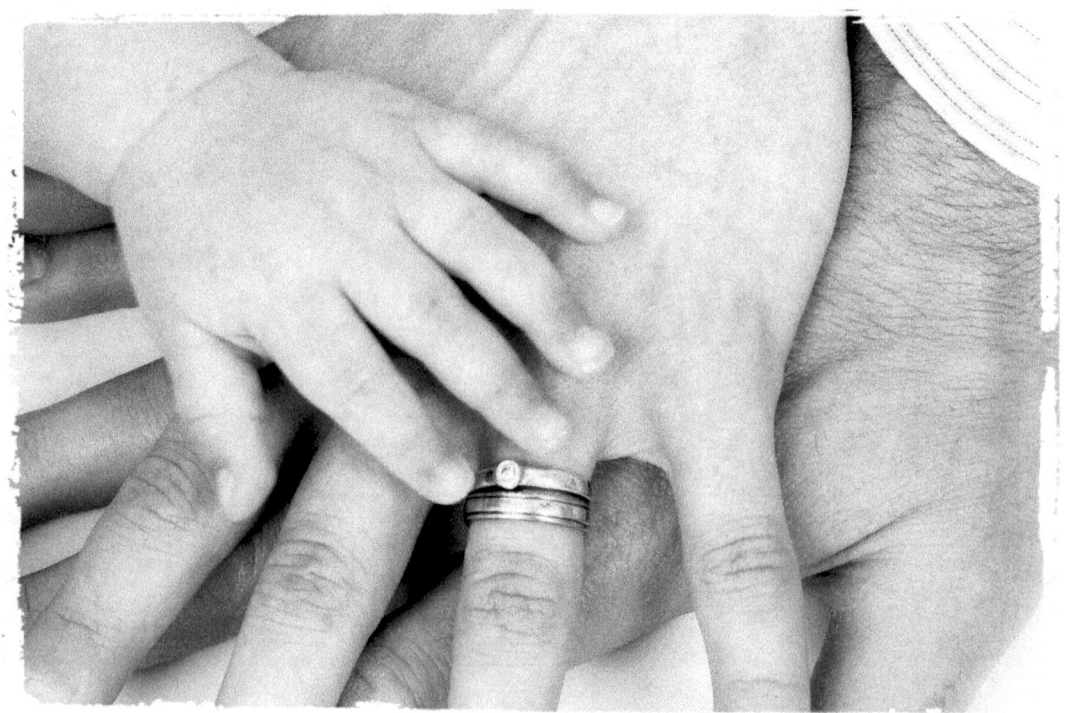

Cliché

cliché
not to be thought
certainly not to be uttered
beneath us
hackneyed
stale –

until it becomes
an arrow shot
right into
the target's center

Then, nothing else fits so well
as this hand-in-glove.

Alas, you are the sand
who slipped through my fingers;
and you, once so palpable,
have left behind
nothing so much as
a single grain of sand.

Convoluted

Ever since we met
I think of you;
I wish to think of you;
I cannot help
but think of you.
However, there is work to do,
so I try not to think of you.
But alas, the effort
not to think of you
(which is considerable)
becomes a way
to think of you.
So I might as well
do as I wish and
think of you,
grateful
that you are so thinkable.

After You Died

Since you died,
even fresh coffee tastes bitter.
I recite Hebrew prayers
in your memory,
mutter fragments of Psalms
that float across my mind.
My gut tightens into a strangle hold;
my body tries in vain to do
what my mind cannot.
Perhaps you have gone
to some Other Side of the universe,
no consolation here.

Since you died,
our familiar melodies enter my mind:
Smetana's "Ma Vlast,"
Dvorak's "Slavonic Dances"
and "Eighth Symphony" –
comforting reminders that keep you near.
Since you died, even my roses
have turned black with grief.
Since you died
I have been unable to cry –
I fear I will drown in my own tears.

Your shadow lengthens
with each passing day.

Life Is Not a Straight Line
for Karam Adibifar

Life is not a straight line;
few paths are direct.
Contingencies rock our intentions.
Euclid is not all there is to life.

An asteroid here, a large meteor there,
a long volcanic night, an ice age —
an amoeba might wonder
how we got here at all.
Life makes wide spirals,
lurches far, then halts,
curves in upon itself.

"Man thinks, G-d laughs,"
goes an old Yiddish saying,
as our line from plans
to results is at best roundabout,
as our plans change in the middle,
and our outcomes stray far from our will.

"Life has no meaning," I said
out of ignorance and arrogance,
when the dots failed to connect
the way I wished
and when I wished them to.

Then, in a moment of grace,
I surrendered to amazement and wonder;
the dots spread out
before me like the Milky Way.
I yielded as an observer
of my own life, and for a moment
no longer needed to connect the dots
into a line of any kind.

Howard F. Stein

Stein, an applied, medical, psychoanalytic, and organizational anthropologist, and organizational consultant, is professor emeritus in the Department of Family and Preventive Medicine, University of Oklahoma Health Sciences Center, Oklahoma City, where he taught for nearly 35 years. He is currently group process facilitator for the American Indian Diabetes Prevention Center, Oklahoma City. He is Poet Laureate of the High Plains Society for Applied Anthropology, and was nominated in 2006 for Oklahoma Poet Laureate. He is author, co-author, or editor of 28 books, of which nine are books or chapbooks of poetry. His poetry is widely published, including in health-related journals. His most recent poetry work is Raisins and Almonds (2014). He can be reached at
~howard-stein@ouhsc.edu
~his Amazon.com page is http://www.amazon.com/Howard-F.-Stein/e/B001HCZ62C

Acknowledgments and Permissions

"Among the Leaves," Harp-Strings Poetry Journal, 25(2) Autumn 2013. P. 17.
"At the Airport Gate," "Awaiting Sundown on the Prairie," Floyd County Moonshine 6(1) Spring 2014: pp. 57, 62 respectively.
"Awaiting the Next Season," "Is There an Earth?" Harp-Strings Poetry Journal 26(2) Fall 2014: Pp. 15, 16, 17 respectively.
"Body Hunger," Pulse – Voices from the Heart of Medicine. 6 May 2016. https://pulsevoices.org/
"Evolution," DoveTales: An International Journal of the Arts, "Nature," 2015: 91-93.
"Geology Lesson," "Cathedrals." miller's pond poetry magazine 19(1) Winter 2016. http://www.millerspondpoetry.com/indexphp/issues/indexphp?page=vol19web1Howard F. Stein Accessed 6 January 2016.
"'Hello!' 'Hello!'," Harp-Strings Poetry Journal 25(4) Spring 2014: p. 17.
"Prairie Farm Photograph," Concho River Review 29(1)Spring 2015: 86
"Sky High – Winter, 2013," Family Medicine 47(9) October 2015: 732. Reprinted with permission of the Society of Teachers of Family Medicine, www.stfm.org
"Sly Hope," "Life Is Not a Straight Line," Families, Systems, and Health 32(2) June 2014: Pp. 247, 250 respectively. Copyright © 2014 American Psychological Association. Reproduced with Permission.
"Spring Procession," Red River Review August 2015. http://redriverreview.net/A55656/rrr.nsf/489dd06eaef-8245f85257e91006ae6/5537... Accessed 23 January 2016.
"The Return," miller's pond poetry magazine 18(3) Fall 2015. http://www.millerspondpoetry.com/index.php/issues/indexphp?page=vol18web3#Howard F. Stein Accessed 1 September 2015.
"The Stream," "Ordinary Miracles," Harp-Strings Poetry Journal (Final Issue) 26(4) Spring 2015: 16-17.
"Transformational Leadership," "Invisible," "Evolution," "Cottonwood Ode," Anthropology Now 7(1) April 2015: 129 ("Transformational...," "Invisible," 130 ("Evolution," "Cottonwood Ode"). Taylor & Francis Group, Publishers.
"Useless Keys," The 40th Annual Oklahoma Conference on Aging Senior Poetry Contest, Oklahoma Department of Human Services, Oklahoma City, OK, p. 111.
"Watch the Winter Wheat," Oklahoma Today. January/February 2014. P. 33.
Photographs courtesy of http://all-free-download.com/

www.ingramcontent.com/pod-product-compliance
Lightning Source LLC
Chambersburg PA
CBHW051423070526
44584CB00023B/3554